THE DARK MOTHERS

THE DARK MOTHERS

Michael Jennings

Copyright © 2020 by Michael Jennings
All Rights Reserved

ISBN: 978-1-7338882-4-0

Manufactured in the United States of America

Black Spruce Press
blacksprucepress.org
blacksprucepress@gmail.com
Design by forgetgutenberg.com
Cover image from the Metropolitan Museum of Art's public domain collection: Marble Female Figure, 2700–2600

CONTENTS

Invocations / 1

The Dark Mothers
    Mary / 15
    Alex / 17
    Lamentations / 32
    The Dark Mothers / 37
    Winter Light / 39
    The Way Out / 42

Dispossessed Creeds and Broken Codes
    Mon Semblable, Mon Frère / 47
    Reading Heaney / 48
    Drum Song / 49
    Lowell / 50
    Talkin' Bob's Blues / 51
    Vilnius Glimpses / 53
    A Dream of Falling / 55

Postscript / 57

INVOCATIONS

Like him, we too have eaten of the word:
with him are somewhere lost beyond the Gorge:
and write, in rain, a letter to lost children,
a letter long as time and brief as love.
—Conrad Aiken, "A Letter from Li Po"

Invocations

My steps slower than I would have imagined
even in summer

who once could not help but run
Crimes I've done myself I would not undo

Cicadas in a tree singing
the dappled 'out there'

the shrill of birdsong

❋

Sands of the desert and sun warm me
and I forgive my pederast father
and remember his shy laugh

Spawn of East Texas swamps snakes on the brain
Stink of rot and piney woods loneliness
Bible-belt mom dowsed in lavender

I had an engineer's hat like my grandfather's
high in the sun-flared locomotive squinting into the light

the two of us until the whistle blew
and he was a crouched old man on a hospital inner tube

My father's bones shattered like glass and he died
worse than a dog so I forgave him

remembering his shy laugh glints of gold
in his long old teeth

Two funny stories maybe three and no one knew him
His skull in death an old Ojibwa's

❃

At night the familiar hocus pocus of moon and mind
You soft in shadow that other
I know myself by

Come Light warm me
Sit on my grandmother's shoulder
who reads me through measles and chickenpox
bringing the world and New Orleans
in two blue suitcases

Light on the banana tree tallest of grasses
Light in her hazel eyes

Salt sand of the desert the long unfolding white of it
Out there I stole my bride from the land of the untouchables
Spirit me away dawn of the cockcrow
Light of my wavering window

My one great photograph you naked on a chaise lounge
eight months pregnant sleeping in the sun
light circling your circles
and one long draped arm

Light of the moment and always

Our son came out a greased chicken when he was born
and shone in the light of all subsequent Christmases

He seemed too small to take home
I had to learn to hold his head up
Your breasts engorged made you the gaudy
fertility goddess carved on a wooden salad spoon
I remembered from childhood

I gave him his first bath
Danced him heart to heart
Happy on the high hill of our summer

And happily I am already dead in a book somewhere
but in the dark closed pages or the light of a window
I don't know

To think I was ever a blank page
a tabula rasa a salt flat
a star

Hold the light at the window I am coming
though my knees ache

I have always enjoyed near the Equator
how sun maps a face
though I live in the snow

I was young in the sun of tennis courts
Pure form and goat mind
fencing the air
before the flat-light green-haze of hospitals
moon men in surgeries
Mother a mirage in the midnight
arriving from Rome

Stars of Paris outside my window
The girl I held in the dark for 13 years
against my loneliness

swims in the sun of the Pacific now
or is dead

I made love on a red cliff over the Mediterranean
at midnight in the cove of Los Pinos
to a woman from another language
beautiful as a mermaid
and hairy as a 23-year-old
I was young dumb in a hurry
No star touched my soul

❈

When I think of light I think of salt flats or snow
though its jewels in the leaves are delectable
and fire your black hair

All these summers I've watched you garden our gold hill
Your hillocks not bad Old Woman
raised like prayer

Names of flowers elude me unless I look them up
Is it the desert in me or a dark mind
that cannot name these belles of light

My first garden was elephant ears and banana trees
and blunt nosed tortoises I kissed on their blunt noses
mossy bricks of the patio
a slight breeze I still recall
on my heat-rashed two-year-old naked buttocks

At three and a ward of the Church
I wanted to bathe with the Deacon's
13-year-old daughter Mary Katherine
because I liked her pubic hair
how it swirled in the warm water
One or two baths and everyone thought better of it
From then on it was Morgan or Hank

And still my life seems strange
I think my lake the Danube sometimes
or remember the pale lime-thick turquoise of the Karoon River
an eel under my left foot
in a shock of wonder

Salt flats and snow and the gardens between

Wherever it was light wanted to go
I said Yo Dis here is America
Let's do-si-do
Dat old Walt Whitman he big he kind
but boring

Which tribe am I
The twang the drawl the Yankee clipper
Which thrum of weathers
Which codes and netherworlds
Which beestings on the tongue

Or is the eye my alibi
and crude syntax

The eye that travels
sees still waves from airplanes
thunderless beaches

In the border towns
of the dead and nearly dead
comes dawn's bleak windows

The casualties were
entirely justified
say the generals

And all that flat line clarity is light

But what of the gutturals of evening
the festooned flesh and ornamental slang
the topsy-turvy muscles of a million mutabilities
carnal carnivals and carnivores
boardwalk bazaar bodega
heartstrings of the tongue's thrumming

when light of the blood is a kind of light

I drummed through the booze jungles of Bangkok
at age 15 door to door whore to whore
till one just 17 took me home to meet the folks
and wash me in the kitchen sink
It was intimate chilling a grim mirror
and in the sickly light of the bare bulb
she was truly beautiful
How much of her may have wished to dance
on my grave I don't know

Angels and vaginas the angels are
vaginas says my sculptor friend in his studio
when I find his new seraphim
stock and static

Stepping back I see it
Yes
if thighs had wings surely we could fly

From a dark declivity a few curlings
broadening into fern fronds
and baroque arabesques
a vertical mouth for a trunk
and the tree of life is any man's wife

❋

And then there were the horses of the sun
ablaze over the clattering rooftops of the world
or at least Khuzistan with its rock hills
and smugglers' trails
A heartbeat between the knees
A breathing like the very wind
Flying the flags of themselves in their girlish manes
the foolishness of all our fathers in their wild eyes

In a monoprint I bought from a friend
three horses graze in a pasture
that might be cloud
the passionless horses of dream or a far field
closer to me now than the horses of wind and fire
muscle and bone
though I miss their salt scent
the rivers of sweat mapping the veins of their necks

Or maybe my friend's print is a dream of horses
dreaming their pastures dreaming their clouds
dreaming the artist dreaming of horses
whose absence is light
around the dark remembered bodies

When my horse the fastest in all Khuzistan died
I was away at college and knew in an instant
my childhood had ended
I tried writing a poem
but couldn't get the Braille of his skin
under my fingers onto the page
He'd lent me the great thunder of his body
and I had lain on his flanks in his stall while he slept
We loved each other with humor like brothers
On the day of our triumph he had blown by
Star of Persia to win by 20 lengths

He nickered and snorted when he heard my footsteps
and when I did not come for months he died
His life blessed mine as only animals can bless
Sometimes our betrayals are mindless as wind
and a man moves emptier than the child that had been

Moon of my mind with your long black hair
Come nearer sit opposite
Let me paint you the girl in the rattan chair
one full breast exposed
one knee drawn up that hides the other
A portrait in shadow but the light of the room

Or now the wise handsome woman Penelope old
whom Odysseus fears taking his eyes off
in his fog of years
The firm cool cheek and coolish eyes
and fires that flicker at night
along her spine

Flesh is not sexy to an old man's eye
until defied by gravity the slightly
slipped buttocks that affirms some pride
the waist loosening its stays
that still has grace
the back that arches that's known some ache
Of course it helps he knew the girl
entwined back in that Ithacan Eden world
neither of them doin nothin
that wouldn't make her mama's hair curl

The song of the desert is the song of oases
the white sand and midnight blue
of Persian Miniatures
In college I took the Luscher Color Test

"not a party game" we played
  as a party game

The colors you chose showed your balance of mind
the book said and I got four asterisks
which meant not even with psychological counseling
would my mind be right

I saw the cultural bias of course
bright yellow and cool green
being the colors of Switzerland on a nice day

I chose burnt orange and a warm brown
the colors "only refugees" had chosen
the colors of Iranian cliff towns

Third I chose a dark blue
which meant according to the book
I used sex to block my fears
of various underworlds and my sense of doom

O well
The pipes of Pan play
as the pipes of Pan do

And it was a midnight blue
the color of oases
the cry of loons

In a glaze of light
the desert men of the high plateau
have faces like worn shoes
Descendants of Alexander's men
their gazes impassive over wide valleys
their stories as cadenced
as Omar Khayyam

Goats jangling like temple bells
they take tea in a circle
talk with their hands
haggling the prices of horses

I know nothing of their wives
or daughters
shadowy sometimes giggly in the doorways

No massing of light on a sundown cliff face
was ever more magical than the changing light
in our son's face

The garden gnome crouching at your side
primed to know name and each thrilling step
of each new planting his voice
of query and awe a small
very silvery bell

His little collie Tommy carved trails
into our deep thickets and taught him the woods
quail raccoon an occasional fox
a big black stray he glowered down
like the wrath of God
He died on one of those trails on a sunny day
at just age 10 with a single yelp
Our son's wail like a knife in the heart
lasted forever

What could I teach him the world
is sometimes like a poem but mostly isn't
Distrust money men corporate slogans pompous diction
The larger he grew the smaller I seemed

Now he has sideburns like Jim Bowie
and slouches in the sun where he walks

We hope he'll learn to think

I wanted to write a poem
whose first line anticipated its last
a box of inevitability
an inevitable box

But life is not like that
Life is a Bob Dylan song
that might go anywhere
or become mumbly and indecipherable

Tramps train whistles a bad sky

We wait for the refrain
Buzzards are circling the bad sky
Tramps enter the train whistles
and then the far blue mountains

But we have faith
Beauty is also circling we think
We wait for the refrain

And there you are again in the garden
after long winter and long years
your sports car body our chiropractor
complains you treat like a truck
your mud wife duds a swatch of black earth
glazing your forehead
radiant
pensive
dreaming garden again out of the squalor
of sticks and mud the sprawled
scrawled skeletons
There's no light I'd rather enter

than this sun on our porch in late March
the bare trees on the far hills rusting with inner fires
the lake ice jagged and scarred
and about to vanish

And we could vanish too Love
become wolves on our ancient hill
our tails still plumed and playful
our eyes still fires

a little blood on the sumac leaves
their wands waving toward a new autumn

THE DARK MOTHERS

*The day departs. It was a seed
of cold light that returned to its pod,
to its dark mother, to be reborn.*
—Pablo Neruda

Mary (1901–1991)

In that city of black iron lace and Gullah talk,
sin sashaying in shadow, I see you walk
down Pirate's Alley, the quick click of your heels
too Episcopal for the tolling of St. Louis's twelve-tongued bells—
a tea rose in a carnival of azaleas—
white-gloved, sky blue, crisp as your forbearers of East Anglia
yet frankly forgiven in the not quite sultry air
of Easter, taken in by the wide river-mouth patois
of slithering shadows on darkened stairs
in just glimpsed courtyards

and swallowed whole in the black rivers of music,
sirening souls, palaces of jazz-joy, the air thick
with spangled night. A slur of voices
and footfalls on the wet-black streets poised
in mid-summer. Bourbon, Decatur, great
boozy names rolled deep in the throat—
a swill of voices
like the night's breeze, tropical, luscious.
And yours in the plush garden of wrought-iron chairs
crackling like a voice on the wireless—
matter-of-fact as a boot sole,
yet fluttering, fluting its thrill
of the just-so.

You were my first mother in that city of flowering nights
and sweating patios. Duplicitous, cunning,
sometimes mad as a hatter,
you undermined your own daughter
to hold me in the tight
niche of your charms—there where Lafitte
strode and Napoleon's death mask
stared ceilingward, I see you flash—
old outlaw in a city of outlaws,
sainted in a city of saints,

"queers," "reprobates." You gave me awe
and madness, a taste for all things stained

and fallen.
You were my New Orleans,
your chasteness the flipside of the stripper's martyred gaze,
the sagging wistful gays
your courtiers, the wisteria your bloom.
Mary, they called you. Mary of the crossword puzzle and
                                                  afternoon
tea, Mary of the rocks, Mary of situations,
whose fall from grace—divorced, shunned,
a bastard grandson and a strident, quick-tongued daughter—
was resurrection in a place of flowers

and music, of terraced talk
on the floating hills of passing nights.
I learned to walk,
your hand in my hand, your electric
voice in my ear.
Even over years, your letters came with the same click
and stutter, your "Angel" signature the relic
of some old family joke
I never quite got.

"The Velvet Bulldozer,"
your doctors whispered near your death.
Your shingles punished you for years,
your retinas detached, your hearing failed.
Only your mind kept ticking in its queer act of will.
In the end, you were vituperative and genteel
as any southern belle. Nurses scuttled.
Doctors deferred. But even their regard
could not hold you forever.
You died with a small sigh—

white in a whited field.

Alex (1929–2001)

1

No act of will or Psychic Hotline cant
can raise you from the "utility urn"
I bought you in from Jern's Crematorium
last week. You're done, Mom, and you shan't
correct my English, nor nothing rail nor rant
against forever more. No high dudgeon
antics can stir the pot. Not even Nieman
Marcus on credit card can make you less than spent.
Farewell to the 12 Minton place settings
you never used, and to the Stickley bed
big as a Roman bath—to the nightshade
and St. John's Wort, masseuse, bed-wettings,
panic calls, blindness—all that pricey dread—
and those who promised love that never came.

2

You were of course the damaged princess, downed
at seven by the osteomyelitis
in your forehead—surgery, leeches,
one eyelid frozen, headaches that would pound
and pound until you saw yourself as drowned
and then redeemed in your own helplessness.
Great doctors mumbled over you like priests
until the divorce lawyers came and found
your miscarrying mother drug addicted,
your rich daddy a secret queer and crazy.
The baffled judge at last left you to choose.
You were just 10. Your breathing grew constricted
and the courtroom walls leaned in. You told me
how the strange tears splashed on your new red shoes.

3

And so you chose the mother you would hate
by 17, who stole your friends and lied
and put on airs, while the new poverty tied
you to yourself like a bad smell. Late
to work one morning in the Gulf Coast heat
after a six-mile walk, you were mortified
to find deodorant on your desk, tied
up with a little ribbon of pure hate.
That was the day, perhaps, you swore off sweat.
Powdered, perfumed, your beauty cool as ice,
you wore a long red coat, stiletto heels.
When, like soft wind, you tucked me in at night
and whisked away into a world of eyes
and mouths and random men, I felt your steel.

4

I hear your sniff of violated privacy
as my man's hands riffle the soft innards
of your long bureaus—folded, layered,
immaculate, lush femininity,
but not quite lacy—wombs of secrecy
that hold old letters in frayed ribbons, half-heard
snatches of conversation like the words
of little girls whose coy hypocrisy
you loathed. Was it your father's shortness made
you crave tall men, with timber in their voices,
who glowered down at me like men on stilts?
Was it just irony the man you married
stood only five foot six and favored boys.
Still I hear the venom of your hissing silks.

5

"Jarvis, Elizabeth Alice," your great
grandmother, slips from a bottom drawer,
faded but lovely as a long-pressed flower,
at perhaps 17. I contemplate
her unstrung collar. She was maybe late
to come in for the photo session hour,
her hair windblown, a breathless now or
never slight parting of the lips. Her fate
was to become an itinerant schoolmarm,
revered for high intelligence and wit,
who married a young minister and raised
three daughters of a certain bearing, charm,
humor and piety. What doesn't quite fit
the story, though, are her eyes—wild, slightly crazed.

6

What tamed that wild gaze that did not tame yours—
the cold Michigan farm?—anxieties
by candlelight?—the sleepless ministries
to endless household needs? From bottom drawers
they all come tumbling out, the ancestor
church ladies. Your grandmother's diaries,
chock full of weather's cheery godliness,
tell nothing of herself, only her prayers
to better serve. They warmed the glittering ice
of those heartbreaking farms that made you cringe,
if family jottings be believed. White haired,
bleak boned daughters of the mad-eyed Alice,
they show up faded at the faded edges
of family picnics—wistful, shyly proud.

7

Your existential loathing of the family
tree came early. One minister seduced
proved quite enough. Even old "Elder" Brewster
of the Mayflower hung there in the leafy
branches your mother grew like Blake's Poison Tree.
Its roots were Charlemagne and Robert Bruce,
the Black Douglas and John of Gaunt. No half-truth
was squandered in her quest for ancestry
of might and merit. You were the poor daughter
who'd never measure up to that high-flown bunk
and didn't try. You sang your own mantra.
You were no Mary Ann, let alone "Junior."
You were no pious chip off the old stump.
You changed your name to Alexandra.

8

Not the carpool mother who sang I Like
Ike songs. Not the girl damaged by her father
who could not say no but not quite yes either.
Not she who made little me one May night
with a blond Mick prize-fighter without quite
conceiving what went on in the weeds there.
Not the petulant, angry daughter,
or even the bad mother or bad wife.
You wanted to exist uncategorically.
You wanted to be an original
created in the diamond moment. Not
for you the pain of being only
one woman. You desired to be impossible,
and stirred and stirred and stirred and stirred the pot.

9

You loathed your mother's wheeler-dealer lies.
She worried you could *be* but could not do—
and always two stories of what was true—
yours and hers, hers and yours in perfect symmetry—
her outward quest, your inward journey,
clashing like cymbals. Both your winds could woo
me. I just saw varying shades of blue—
you darker and she lighter, but the same sea.
You both loved words, and words kept you apart.
In the same room, I'd feel your grinding wills
like creaking oarlocks, both a little crazy
and both killed off by the same bad heart.
You read Proust. She read me Wordsworth's "Daffodils."
In different climes, you each got called "a lady."

10

You toyed with me with threats of suicide
that year I turned 11. Even then
I thought you were just putting me on
at least half the time. But of course I cried
and rubbed your back, and in my own way tried
to wrestle down your darkest demons
as if you were my double. And just once
I feared you'd kill me in my sleep—some tired
hotel in Switzerland as I recall.
We'd fought. You had been drinking pretty hard.
But I remember mostly how the lake
was blue as lapis and we were immortal.
The incident left us drifting apart.
We just let it alone for beauty's sake.

II

All family wars play out best with three.
"What can we do with Alex, what's anyone
to do with Alex," Grandmother would intone
when I was fourteen and thought life easy.
We'd settle in for a long night's breezy
confession of your sins. Crazy as a loon
sometimes, she had the storyteller's one
virtue—to forge some actuality
just as she forged diplomas that got her work.
You were the poor poet of introverted
glances, who saw not things but in their ideas
that fluttered mothily toward the Absurd.
For you communion lurked behind the words.
After dissecting you, we'd have our *brioche*.

12

You showed no great interest in your grandson
and hated any grandmotherly role.
The very appellation seemed to appall
you, as if threatening your sense of fashion
and proper distance. No cuddly fat munchkin
hugger you. It was all about control
and self-possession and your ghastly will.
The touch you craved was near another ocean
under the calm fingers of your masseuse.
What you could buy you could put trust in—
even to that huge, somber library
whose books you never bothered to peruse.
You were just out there like the last Victorian
dying amidst some phantom tea party.

13

With enough money nothing need be real.
You blew through seven hundred thousand,
a grand a month for your group psychic plan
alone. The rest, just baubles of the *haute* genteel—
Cartier clocks, drawers full of identical
designer suits in three sizes, not one
worn—scarves and sweaters numberless as sand,
and so on. Mostly it was pretty dismal
being you those last years, ordering things
through UPS to have a moment's friend
when packages arrived. Your eyes were failing
and liver functions—clear rememberings
of things that had not ever happened.
The sirens in your blood-starved head were wailing.

14

When it was clear the money had run out,
quite willessly you fell upon your sword,
refusing Laesix that your doctor ordered
and losing him for that. For one coquette
moment you tried to call a quick about
face, change your mind. Nurses were guarded—
it was too late now for that. You looked bored
and drifted back to sleep. And that was that.
Your new friend-cosmetician held your hand.
Another startled as she entered your room
and one bright blue eye held her in its death-chill.
There was no code blue or shenanigans.
You'd become bride to yet another groom.
The angry child kicking in your head lay still.

15

Your portraits we brought home filled several boxes—
from Shirley Temple days to the young Hepburn,
your slightly cocked head and cocked eyebrow turn
the gaze inward, despite the outward glances
at the demanding camera. Long eyelashes
veil the quick bright eye. Something flickers and burns
and smolders out. A certain porcelain
veneer distracts us from your beauty's darkness.
What you held dearest was your inner kingdom.
In most all the portraits, that shows up.
None of them hold the look I cherish—
that devil-may-care, slightly-over-the-top,
what-the-hell grin. That wink. It all said come
dance, little broody boy, it's all there is.

Lamentations

Lament 1

I sat on the edge of my bed and I wailed and I wept
and I wanted to be empty as wind
and avoid all this old man dying shit
all this piecemeal dissolution humiliation
I wanted to rise like the Phoenix like the sun
and be new in the morning like the sun
I wanted to be 56 forever everything still
almost possible you like a mirage
just ahead within reach a rainbow's
shimmering I wanted to walk in
content in my fate to be walking still walking
the ache in my knees both telling and reassuring
and you in the paper tiara from the party
Queen May aswirl in the ribbons of mock death
and resurrection and I knew making love
to you would make me whole through the universe
and everything else the denouement the terrible denouement
weeping and keening holding the rags the bitter rags
and then I was empty as wind and quiet

Lament 2

I went to the place of the poem but it was small
and dark and smelled like the ancient dens of foxes
Time kept coming back to scratch at the door
Old words littered the walls as if to keep the damp out
Someone had lit a fire but the ashes were cold
and the spiders were everywhere
And there was such sadness in the spaces between words
so much nothingness in the everything they said
Why fear the nothingness but we do
How fear the meaninglessness which we are
Here is my voice hang it on a tree
Here is my shoe which remembers me
And beautiful were your black diamonds
like the beauty of the sea at night
the points and spires and breezes of the night
where you passed and I followed and the words went out
and I vanished

Lament 3

I wanted to steal the last word from Death I suppose
and the silkiest of thefts are the poems of moonlight
poems of the sea and vast deserts their premonitions
And yet the Angel of Death is all kindness we're told
leading us out into moonlight through cracks in the clouds
had we known had we listened as the terrible talons
of pain and undoing let go
                        let us pray let us hope
the last ravening moments no end of consciousness
but a beginning
                   let us hope let us pray
though your buttocks domes against my limp gizmo
are all I need tonight to shore me home

Lament 4

How shall I say goodbye to myself poor
Charles Bon in his New Orleans and his emptiness
his decadence and charm and poisonous knowledge
who yet found you beyond all luckiness or fate
Goodbye to the heart hurt by its own betrayals
the mind full of inconsequence and error
a voice too full of itself
knickknacks and charms and the color blue
the silent cries of trees and the lake's sheen
and the numberless leaves haunting the numbered days
The man of the hour is the skeleton in the sombrero
who lies down in the curves of the voluptuous senorita
to a clatter of bedpans in the wings and the cackling of the damned
I sang you the songs of your fiery bones
and the soft opening flower of a dying kiss
Farewell to the grief of days and the holy smell of roses
your face knees voice like water
thighs like snow and eyes full of sky
Your laugh startled me so so so long ago
My will such as it is I give to clouds and to dreaming
my bones to the cathedrals of sand
to the pottery shards of lost places
my eyes to the vulture who resembles me
my wishes to wind and my loneliness
to thousand-year-old trees and the deserts of desire
I loved you in the simplest of ways my girl
and this is my poem which has no ending

Lament 5

I can imagine the loneliness of widows unraveling
unwelcoming days and old men in shut rooms
measuring their meds losing their minds dates names
If only vanishing were easy an old movie maybe
the corny deathbed speech the melodrama
each bedside mourner a cameo and case study
You see it in the eyes the soul speaking eye to eye
for the last time drinking the last horizon
And the faces strange and the rooms we wake in
with a start the floor moving and the windows dark
are no more ours than the clouds are or the voices of children
Is it the book misplaced that makes me weep
or tortured animals slaughtered children rape
by bayonet or any gone world's going
My grandmother kept a book 85 years pressing
a four-leaf clover given by a friend when they were five
Isn't that worth more than walking on the moon
but nothing stays still straight or in place
but the mute dignity of bones
bones without memory bones without song
So let us go under the hill and over the sky
and let us be bones together

The Dark Mothers

are wailing for their lost sons.
For them little has changed since Moses
but the weapons. A grief ago, the desert wind,
the on and on relentless drone

of once soft women in the murmuring grass,
now crones of the hard afternoon light—
lizard skin and hands become bird claws,
unforgiving eyes, like the mirrors of time,

keening out of the dark towns of my past
the dirges of the young undone
in their animal prime, the I-in-eye
vanishing in the caldrons of oblivion
where once Zarathustra dreamed.

I planted for the goddess some small conifers
now taller than our house and touching the stars,
one a great monster swaying in the moonlight
like the headdress of Shiva
swaddling a dozen birds, a million crawling things.

Together we dance on forgetfulness
and the clouds become elephants.
So this is old age, where the light splinters and the dream
ricochets, and the so-what bird laughs
like Rembrandt's last self-portraits.

(But the poet wants only to speak of sky and the ocean
of sand, to point to the setting sun
with a shrug of indifference.)

✳

The weight of the dead is in the weightlessness
of the vanished who gave you dimension.
The 8th-grade teacher with a Boston accent
who says repeatedly don't call me ma'am,
the east Texas "mammy" with a face like Louis Armstrong
who carries in her sainted flabby arms
the first skewers of guilt and self-loathing,

and so on and so on with the vanishing weight of being,
the slow dissolution of knowing and caring—

the stone door, the widow's wail,
the click of the lid.

And so she brings fire to the ragged dark
in the flare of her hipbones,
swirl of her thighs. Tapering fingers
seamstress nimble, spidery smooth.

And now your absence glows
in the vaults of her belly, toss of her hair.
The slippery dark dances. But already
she is elsewhere, tomorrow
or yesterday, phantom of your best self
curling into smoke—dawn inventing the near hills,
the charred black of your face bones

wobbling back into morning.

Winter Light

> *Like a long-legged fly upon the stream*
> *His mind moves upon silence.*
> —W. B. Yeats, "Long Legged Fly"

He was only the pale winter light
listening. He was old.
The woman had come, shimmering
like a tree reflected in water, and given him eyes.
Now she was fading back into forest
where he could not follow. She hated
his dreary naps, lies. Eternity yawned
into the wavering salt flats of his youth
that had meant distance and loneliness
and something he could not name,
yawned into the land of the dead
where all the old ghosts stood like statuary
with no need for names. His mind
the black edge of a crow's wing,
it had been a long winter, a white desert.

He was listening.

          Armies on the move again
and the rice bowls empty. Bodies in the mountains,
bulging in rivers. A small man, unhoused
in a small boat, trying to save his skin.
In the palace a little wine under the indifferent
beauty of sky, a little sex, a little death.
And the stink of it, rape and the mad dance
among fires.
        Li Po trudging the hills far from home.

As if the sky itself were sluicing down
into their slumberous bodies: blue horses

in an orange field ablaze in late sun,
a kind of paradise of the moment, out of time
and therefore holy. At the edge of the field
a shadow, the menace of time. Or is it
the face with many lines gazing from the window
into the fragrance of horses, the draped manes
and long faces of peace in the grass, skin
that rippling makes the whole body smile.
The woman had shown him this, in her broad hips
and liquid thighs, the chime of her laugh.

He imagined the up-thrust cathedral's burden of stone
poised impossibly on a mathematical notion,
moonlight streaming down through the clerestory—
all that blood-soaked stone aching to be light,
or if not light, wings—
voices glancing off stone muffled in the tall air,
officious whisperers, assorted saints, She
off in a corner encaved in her forest of stone,
only the Mother of God now,
not of the trees and grass.

The Oneidas tell their stories only in winter
so that the snakes who hide behind leaves
cannot hear them—the way poems are made
so the thugs lurking behind walls
with their electronic gadgetry
grow blank as river stones.
In dreams I return to the hill people's
fires and drum circles, speaking my poems
to the dark full of sparks and fireflies.
A woman lay down like a black river there
in the moonlight drunk with poets.

He came on the rank river of swarming humanity
and beautiful ochres
to the gold temple with its leafy chimes
pearling the air like the voices of insect angels—
the pumpkin headed, pumpkin colored monks
anonymous as flowers—
a place of exact thoughtlessness
stirred by a single tremulous note
like the smile of the sky itself.
Overhead in the voluptuary trees,
the white fanged, long tailed gods and goblins
chuckling like monkeys—
in the time before time in the reign of the tiger.

He dreamed these things as the wind blew and the cold deepened
and the shadows behind his face
became a gathering of crows arguing with evening—
each caw a vanishing soul, each coal-black eye
ironic and insolent. Praise be
to the nefarious crow—carrion eater,
squawker, complainer—
Praise be to our allotted cup of blood.

The Way Out

How It Started: The Train Station

I was leaving the comfortable nest and warren life
of the shadowy French Quarter
when the great clanking, screeching, spark-spitting
dragon locomotives
set me dancing as if on hot coals
behind my mother's wide familiar skirts
as I learned the beginning of displacement is fear
67 years ago
like yesterday

a residual bubble on the river of I

The long dead haunt me
who were the beautiful women
of my half-orphaned childhood
gliding naked in the bathroom steam
like Olympians, my mother's rosy nipples,
my grandmother's dark areolas
in the paradise of innocence.
Now even their bones are powder,
their spirits only the mists of my brain
and vanishing.

In the middle ground tortured mountains under the ache of sun.
Long bray of the donkey in the valley of yesterday.
Ululating mothers. Dark
laughter. And who are you in the foreground
trying to take stock like a man in fog
in his circle of lantern light. The 50-year story of a worsening limp.

To walk out into the sun and not come back
is the promise of the desert,
the dream of its wavering lakes.
I now know more dead than living says my rolodex,
numbers I'll never call again: dear detritus.
I'm looking for the whisper
that says this matters
among the battering bartering voices
seeking their moment of importance,
their 15 seconds of resonance,
the moments between this and that
when the doors to our souls stand open
and waiting.

I've been reading young men long dead
to decipher my ambiguous handprints.
They are neither here nor there,
my brothers in solitude, and a few sisters
who help me float. It's their floating I'm after
and a few feathery hints. I'm now. I'm not.
On/off. The flickering neon of a flung down
grunge country strip-joint under enormous
star-studded sky. The gone-ness of it all.
The space. The closeness.
How small we are
and grand.

Time fans out in too-rich technicolor again
the tulip fields of Holland in a dollhouse world
with tiny wooden bridges,
my motorcycle throbbing like a heart,
like a plundering dynamo,
like thunder.

I was a demi-demon riding the thunder
in a dollhouse world.

The living echo summons the lost body like a voice in a dream.
Walking in a hiss of rain on a roadway
a recalcitrant ghost, the everyman slouch of resistance.
Through the trees a glistening lake,
an eye peering up from the underworld
amazed and amazing. We search for the rainbow.
We hunt for ourselves. We honor the sun.

I believe in the God of Hafez, sky
becoming woman becoming sky again,
great stretch of the infinite scented with rosewater
or orange blossoms in a shady bower.
I have ridden that sunbeam
of summer gold and the moonbeams
of silent adoration, my body
now an old leather coat I must soon take off
 to enter the summoning river of absence.

And the sky is not empty but open
says the dead poet who stands in for us all
in this poem of slippery slopes
and kneeling grass,
glittery shards and non-sequiturs.

The sky is not empty but open.

DISPOSSESSED CREEDS AND BROKEN CODES

Artists are the Indians of the white people.
—Lame Deer

Mon Semblable, Mon Frère
for K.S.K.

Old Oily Bones crouching in the Ganges' mud
or sauntering up our drive, Tequila and peppers
proffered like flowers, I feel your shadow
lurking in corners months after you depart—
broken-down Caddy asputter.
                         We drink late,
spout poems and oaths, feel the sun rise
through bleached bones, know the same curse
blesses as the stones are blessed, as Tequila is blessed
and the tongue is a shrine.
                         We swell with the pride
of Flamenco swagger, ride the old blues uncouth
truth and parody, feel the universe
slide through us.
                         You're gone in a swill of rucksacks
and vagabond luggage, crazy patois,
leaving us waving down the drive.
                         The day
is full of patches of sun, on the counter,
across the desk, shadows in the gold grass,
as I feel you retreating
                         back into the tall Pennsylvania timber,
head down, long strides, back into the long silence
of unmade poems and gypsy songs.

Reading Heaney

No need to get carried away the voice
says meaning there'll be time enough for that

life anyway a slow leak back into
stars from that first edge-of-the-world place

bog-rooted and hedged in cow-quivering sleet
and the imperative to keep weather out

along with such novelties and courtesies
and verities of tongue as horse traders use

language come up to look men in the eye
across the pasture gate and slow reticence

of educated hands attaching fact
to fact all the way back to the Bog Woman

in her death necklace—
                        though the boy looks out
enthralled by the imperative of dawn

to stop thinking to start it all again—
hear the poem knotted up in the sheep's bleat

or the valley's clattering first hooves of light

Drum Song
        in memory of Ted Hughes

The lightning-flashed hag face of the moor
in the torpor of downpour
and the drizzle-dim skull of Heptanstall

and the curse in the blood of the cursed mud
and Heathcliff's Mother-wound horror
put thistle in the tongue of Yorkshire

the crashing shires and long haul of mountains
where rock and wind ate at each other
and ached for each other like star-crossed lovers

fossilized in poems whose undersong
was the silkiest hands of farmers
coaxing at the womb door

and the galloping gaiety of the otter
slipping his pelt like a sorcerer
and the river's unkillable contradictions and seasons

her unkillable children and thunder

in the big double drum of the heart

Eros/Thanatos   Eros/Thanatos   Eros/Thanatos.

Lowell

> *In the old New York, we said*
> *"If life could write,*
> *it would have written like us."*

You lost your arid God, His dragon tail
and gorgeous plumage whipping the sea swell
of your Promethean will and thunder
in your "all percussion" obit for the Quaker—
manner or matter your evolving question—
the boy-Keats muscled to the nearly German.

What then? The down look and the letting go,
whiskey glazed eye in false-gold afterglow,
the soft patter of friends no longer pattering,
snippets, smatterings,
crisscrossed conscience and coincidence,
the world's crush
crumpling in a handkerchief—
as if the daze of old age were all day
in a deckchair's decadent complicity
or child's play.

I like the last poems best, their blurry wonder
and disconnects...
the Boston Brahmin with the southern drawl,
vernacular still sparring for the jugular...
the convalescent back from rehab...
seafarer
come home in a New York cab.

Talkin' Bob's Blues

You can't get there from here though you can go a lot of places
In the switchyard of the mind you can rearrange a lot of faces
But the scent of her hair and the touch of her lips and the curse of her tongue
Say you'll bleed from your eyes till the day you're done

When the plains' red dawns stretch out like lies
And the cut glass of the past gives you spider web eyes
And you feel like you're crawling through the land of the dead
And know the dream of your life should have stayed home in bed

And you don't wanna do what beauty asks
Though she's always there in the mirror's masks
Jean Genet in the role of town crier
Or the vagabond king disguised as vampire

Or the ragamuffin boy who could be anyone
Hank or Woody or the scourge of the sun
Deranging the world to see for the first time
Mississippi was a state of mind
And Desolation just a street sign

You can't get there from here though you jump through hoops
You can dance on the clouds or you can deal from the stoops
Your mama had a sister her sister had a friend
She wanted to bust out he wanted to keep it in
And a baby's cry is the willow's wind
You can't even pray without some kind of sin

Walk down the backstairs slip off in the dark
The devil's face is Joan of Arc's
We might be 40 miles outside of somewhere
But the locals say you can't get there from here

Smoke's been travelin' all through the swamps
Says the trees have been whisperin' the words of Mein Kampf

Innocence cries in even the darkest heart
You can die for a rose or you can die for art
And all kinds of things that were wrong from the start

I got a woman behind my door
Says she'll love me but I gotta be poor
Gotta crawl on my knees gotta howl like a dog
But if I'm a prince she'll make me a frog

You can't get there from here though you toss and you turn
And your dreams get heavy and your eyes start to burn
But there's a place you can get to on down the road
Where lying's just another kind of truth in code

And an old man playing a Chinese flute
Says I've had mine you can take the loot
The white beard of nothingness grows from my chin
And the next time we meet we'll all be kin

There's a place I go about a mile from here
Where I take off my face and examine my fear
The lake shines like a mirror and I cup my ear
And nothing much matters but that the words are clear

There are freight cars passing and old crossroads
And dispossessed creeds and broken codes
And dead end dreams where a life implodes
And sometimes you see her dancing in fire
But you can't sing her back from the land of desire

You can bray like a donkey you can caw like a crow
There are some kinds of places words can't go
He went down in the valley to sing his song
And let the echo decide if he was right or wrong

He let the echo decide if he was right or wrong

Vilnius Glimpses
        For Kornelijus Platelis

In the lonely room of the poem

(sifting
plaster dust
and spreading wall
maps of moisture
in the slow
garlic-sour crumble
of old Europe)

the heavy-faced poet ponders the book of losses
dreaming redemption
from the irony and ache of arthritis

or maybe the clatter and clash of sun-bright weapons
as the pagan suicide knights of the forest
vanish into the blood-smoke incense
of the crucifix

but no let up in the relentless walk of the world
eyes dead ahead
ghosts of the mind cops and word killers

and too little mystery or amnesia
in a quart of *degtine*

no matter the glassy glitter of boutiques
no matter the smart fashion-girls with their cell phones
and small taut buttocks

and the roaring poets of cavernous taverns
blinking into the sun
to mumble poems like apologies
in the still sacred tongue of oak and linden

and placating shrines to the gothic gods of unmaking—
rampant St. George plunging
his lance into the waiting mouth of the monster
and interchangeable saints
wilting like flowers

I want to go home to make love
to my beautiful wife
on the timeless hill of our dreams
stolen from the Iroquois

I want to tear out my teeth in the soundproof
torture chambers of the KGB
and forget the cool-eyed women cut down
in the demystified forest
like a thousand Dianas

I want words to unsay themselves
and the clocks to stop

I want to drink till I drop
and sleep in the gutter
with the rain leaking into my brain
and be washed in the blood
of inscrutable gutturals
and make a friend of sorrow and terror

I don't want to be written into the heavy book
of the poet with his bitter grief
and Sphinx-like gaze
knowing it all might have been otherwise

though our eyes have met
and there's no going back

A Dream of Falling
        in memory of Karl Wallenda

He slept perhaps
the way Sherpas
on a long climb
sleep: on the move,
as though the mountain
were mere dream and the next step
all that mattered: a hole
pushed into the nothing
that it might vanish
into nothing
and leave him to wake refreshed.

He woke to a dream
of falling. If there was a scream
it came from another room. It was not
his. He was too transfixed
to scream. He had dreamed the dream
too often.
        But then he had not come
to conquer the mountain. He had done that
years ago: wooed it and brought it to his bed
like a woman. Now he came to the mountain
as a mountain, and dreamed of a man
falling, a man gone suddenly womanish
and expansive, opening his body to sky,
accepting it, as the mountain does, with open arms.

POSTSCRIPT

Although I trust it will make no difference to the reading experience of this book, it is the last of a quartet of books that included *Summoning the Outlaws, Where She Dances,* and *The Moon's Children,* exploring the landscapes and dreamscapes of my life as I have been able to conjure them, sculpt them, trick them into place: sacred places that seem now to have always been there but needed the nudge and whisper of the muse, who *got* where I needed to go, breathed life into the spirits I needed to dance with, and masqueraded as my remarkable wife for over 40 years, acting as both editor and auditor through all the stages of what Donald Hall called Goatfoot, Milktongue, and Twinbird, those most elemental aspects of the ancient art of poem-making.

www.ingramcontent.com/pod-product-compliance
Lightning Source LLC
Chambersburg PA
CBHW021132080526
44587CB00012B/1254